TASTE

A TRUE BOOK®
by
Patricia J. Murphy

Children's Press®
A Division of Scholastic Inc.

New York Toronto London Auckland Sydney
Mexico City New Delhi Hong Kong
Danbury, Connecticut

A young girl enjoys
the taste of her pasta.

Reading Consultant
Nanci R. Vargus, Ed.D.
Assistant Professor
Literacy Education
University of Indianapolis
Indianapolis, IN

Content Consultant
Beth Cox
Science Learning Specialist
Horry County Schools
Conway, SC

Dedication:
For my mother,
With love P.J.M.

Library of Congress Cataloging-in-Publication Data

Murphy, Patricia J., 1963–
    Taste / by Patricia J. Murphy
    p. cm — (A true book)
    Summary: Explores the sense of taste and the body parts used to pro-
duce it as well as its relationship to smell.
    ISBN 0-516-22600-2 (lib. bdg.)   0-516-26971-2 (pbk.)
    1. Taste—Juvenile literature. [1. Taste. 2. Senses and sensation.] I. Title.
II. Series.
QP456 .M875 2003
612.8'7—dc21

2001008383

Contents

Your sense of taste begins to work as soon as food or drink reaches your tongue.

It Tastes So Good!

Grab a sandwich and take a bite. When you bite into it, your mouth starts chewing, crunching, and swallowing. Before you swallow, something rather "tasty" happens. With every bite of food or sip of drink you put into your mouth, you taste. To taste food, your tongue and taste buds must work together. A message from your tongue must travel to your brain as well.

Taste is one of your body's most enjoyable senses. With your sense of taste, you can taste thousands of flavors. Without it, food would be boring to eat. You might never want to eat anything again. Your body might not get the foods it needs to be healthy or to grow. Your sense of taste makes sure this

Without taste, you might lose interest in eating.

Food is the fuel that helps your body function.

does not happen. Because of taste, your body enjoys eating. This joy allows you to feed your body.

Your sense of taste also helps protect you from harm. Taste can protect you from eating many rotten or poisonous things. If you've

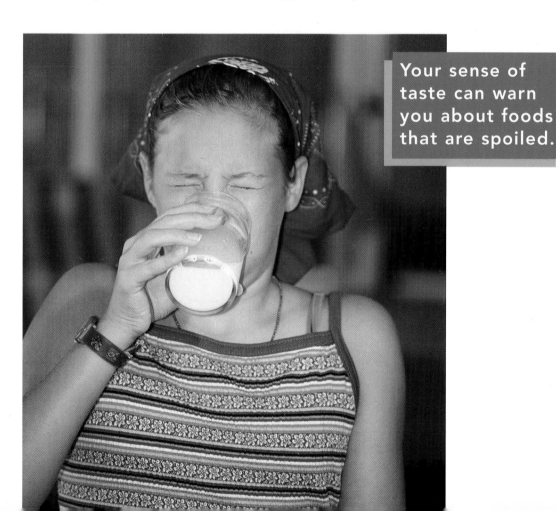

Your sense of taste can warn you about foods that are spoiled.

ever sipped milk that has gone bad, you know how awful it tastes. You might gag or need a drink of water to get the taste out of your mouth.

Most tastes are good tastes. Sometimes, you can't seem to get enough of certain tastes! You can't wait to chew, crunch, slurp, and swallow some foods. Before you swallow, you get to taste them. Tasting begins with your tongue.

For many people, popcorn
is a very tasty snack.

The Tongue

When you stick out your tongue, you'll see only part of it. Your tongue is a group of muscles. The muscles begin in the front of your mouth and stretch to the back of your throat.

Your tongue has different tasks. First, your tongue allows

There's more to your tongue than you can see.

you to form sounds like "LLL" and "TTT." The tongue also helps you to speak and ask important questions, such as "What's for lunch?"

Your tongue helps your body's **digestive system** too. Your tongue holds on to the food and moves it around in your mouth. This helps your teeth cut and chew your food. Together, your tongue and teeth help turn your food into wet, round balls.

Like a wild roller coaster, your tongue moves the food balls. These balls move up, down, and all around the small bumps on your tongue. These bumps are called **papillae**. They are different shapes.

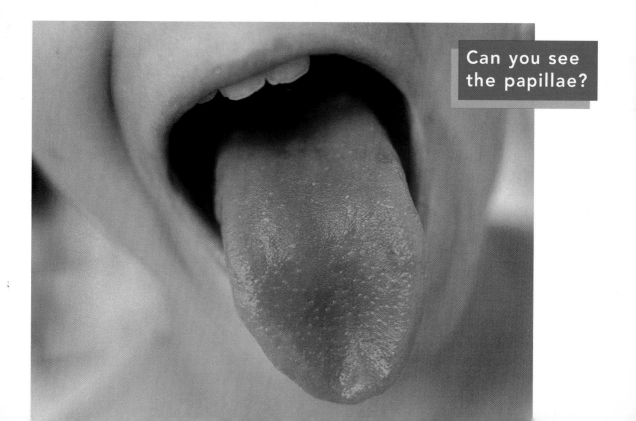

Can you see the papillae?

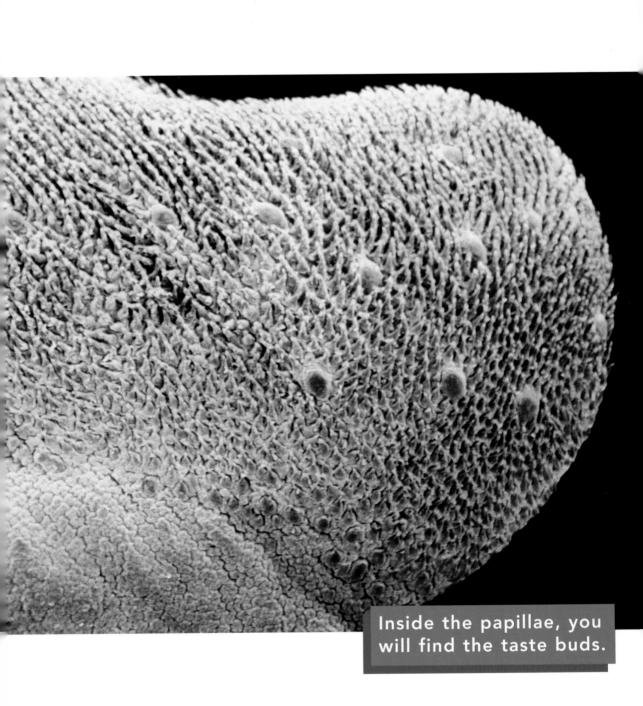

Inside the papillae, you will find the taste buds.

You can see your own papillae. Just stick out your tongue and look in the mirror. You should see the little bumps. Inside these little bumps are your body's taste buds. These taste buds are balls of **nerve cells** or receptors. Some papillae have only one taste bud. Other papillae may contain as many as 250 taste buds.

The Taste Buds

Under a microscope, your bumpy tongue looks like a mountain range. Your taste buds looks like flower buds. That is how taste "buds" got their name!

Some scientists believe that the tongue has four taste areas—sweet, salty,

This close-up photograph shows two different kinds of papillae. The small papillae are called filiform and the larger, round ones are called fungiform.

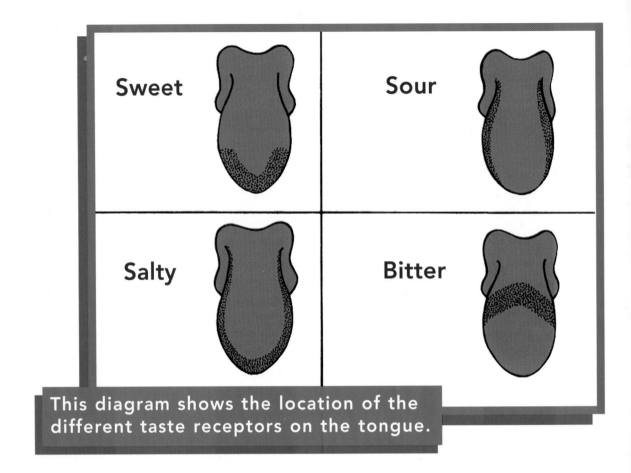

Sweet

Sour

Salty

Bitter

This diagram shows the location of the different taste receptors on the tongue.

sour, and bitter. They believe the sweet and salty taste areas are found in front of your tongue. Sour and bitter taste areas are in the back.

Other scientists believe that all of the tongue's taste buds can taste many different tastes. Still others believe there is a fifth taste. This taste is called "meaty." It can be found in Japanese and Chinese meals.

Some scientists believe that there is a fifth type of taste called meaty. You can experience this taste by trying Chinese or Japanese food.

When food moves across your tongue's taste buds, you can sense a combination of tastes or flavors. To actually taste something, your body's **saliva**, or spit, helps to break down your food into chemicals. These chemicals fill a pore, or hole, in the top of each taste bud. The chemical starts the taste buds' tiny nerve cells and their hairs moving. This tells the nerve

cells to send out **nerve
impulses**, or messages.

First, these nerve impulses
run along the nerve cells'
paths, or **nerve fibers**. Next,
they travel through the taste,
or gustatory, nerves. These
nerves carry the messages
to the middle of your brain.
There, the brain sorts out
the different messages.

Once the messages are
sorted, they travel on to the
parietal lobe of the cerebral

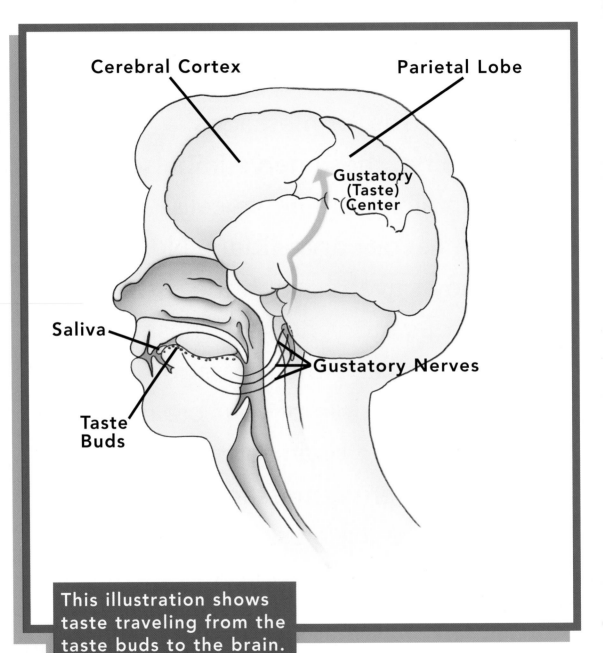

Cerebral Cortex

Parietal Lobe

Gustatory (Taste) Center

Saliva

Gustatory Nerves

Taste Buds

This illustration shows taste traveling from the taste buds to the brain.

cortex. This lobe is the taste, or gustatory, center of the brain. The gustatory center is where the brain identifies thousands of tastes. Of all the senses, taste has the longest journey to make to reach the brain. Like eating your favorite meal slowly, it is worth the wait.

Time Line of Taste Buds

Babies have more taste buds than adults do. They like sweet things, such as milk and fruit.

Babies lose some of their taste buds as they get older.

Babies enjoy sweet foods and drinks.

You probably developed many of your food preferences from your family.

Children learn to like the foods their families eat. They get used to different foods and spices.

As children become adults, they try new tastes. They make their own food choices.

When people get older, around the age of seventy, their taste buds grow back more slowly. They may taste less. Their sense of smell grows weaker too. These people might use more salt and sugar to season their food.

Taste and Smell

Your sense of taste relies on your tongue and your taste buds. It also relies on your nose. Scientists believe that the sense of taste is actually 75 percent smell.

As you chew your food, smell molecules, or particles, break off from the food you

Your sense of smell plays a significant part in how you taste things.

Take a bite of a sandwich. Once the food is in your mouth, messages about how the sandwich smells travels to your brain.

eat. They travel to the back of your throat and up to your **nasal cavity**. There, they cause your olfactory, or smell, organ's nerve cells to start sending smell messages to your brain.

At the same time, food molecules are mixed with your saliva. This liquid causes your taste buds' nerve cells to send impulses to your brain. When these smell and taste messages are processed by your brain, you smell and taste your food. Together, your senses of taste and smell allow you to identify and enjoy many flavors.

When you have a cold or allergies, you cannot smell.

Being sick can really lessen your ability to taste.

You also cannot taste. The nasal passages become red, swollen, and thick with mucus. Smell molecules cannot reach the nose's olfactory organ. No smell messages can be sent to the brain. You have trouble breathing and smelling. Your food has little or no taste. Once the cold or allergy is gone, you can smell and taste again.

People who take certain medicines sometimes experience a loss of taste. Some people report

Some medicines can affect your sense of taste.

that they have a metallic taste in their mouths. Others just notice that things taste bland or plain.

Hot and cold foods can affect your sense of taste. These foods can even damage taste buds for a while. Head injuries can also hurt the taste area of the brain. People with brain injuries may lose their sense of taste forever.

Fortunately, taste buds can grow back. Most of the time,

Eating something hot or cold could alter your sense of taste.

taste buds come back quickly. So, taste never really leaves you for very long.

Tasting Ice Cream All Day Long!

John D. Harrison tastes more than sixty packages of twenty different flavors of ice cream each day. His job is to make sure that Edy's Ice Cream has all the right stuff—cream, sugar, and other flavors.

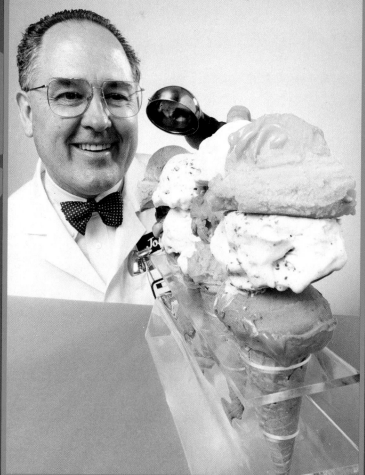

His taste buds can tell if there's too much of one thing or not enough of another. He calls his tasting method "the swirl, smack, and spit."

So far, he has tasted more than 180 million gallons of ice cream! He tells future tasters to "taste foods slowly to notice their differences and study dairy or food sciences!"

Take Care of Your Sense of Taste

Every day, most people wash their bodies and brush their teeth. These are two ways that people can help themselves stay clean and healthy. Your senses of taste and smell need special care too. To help these senses

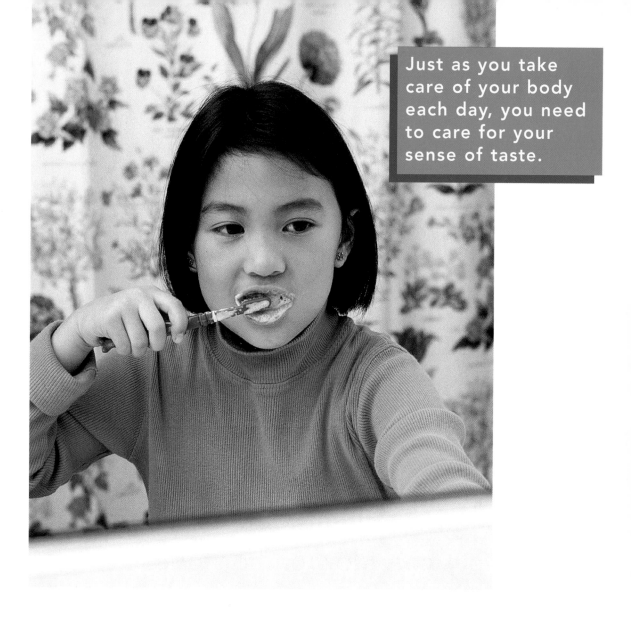

Just as you take care of your body each day, you need to care for your sense of taste.

do their jobs, here are things you can do.

Blowing on food (left) is one way to cool down food that is too hot. It's important to floss every day (right). It keeps food from getting stuck in between your teeth and causing decay.

• Do not eat food when it is very hot. Blow on hot foods and hot drinks or wait for them to cool. Hot temperatures can hurt your taste buds.

• Keep sharp objects away from your tongue. Sharp objects, such as scissors or knives, can damage your tongue and your taste buds. They can also keep the tongue from helping you eat and speak.

• Do not smoke! Smoking can dull your senses and stop you from smelling and tasting things.

• Brush and floss your teeth and gums. Brushing and flossing help keep your teeth and gums healthy. They also keep you from getting gum disease and cavities. These things can also hurt your sense of taste.

• Do not taste or smell unfamiliar things. You could hurt your taste buds and your nose. You might end up getting very sick.

• See a doctor if you have trouble tasting or smelling. Colds and allergies can affect taste and smell. Most times, when colds or allergies go away, taste and smell return.

Facts About Taste

- You have nine thousand or more taste buds on your tongue!

- People who are "supertasters" may have as many as 1,100 taste buds in 1 square centimeter of their tongues.

- Bitter is the strongest of your taste buds.

- Saliva kills germs and keeps your mouth moist. It also helps break down your food.

- The roof of your mouth and the back of your throat have taste buds too.

- Babies even have taste buds on their cheeks! They soon lose them.

- Scientists are working to discover other tastes the tongue can recognize.

- You may like or dislike a food because of how it feels on your tongue or in your mouth.

- Warm drinks taste sweeter than cold drinks.

- Cold temperatures increase bitter tastes.

To Find Out More

Here are additional resources to help you learn more about the sense of taste.

 **Books**

Cobb, Vicki. **Your Tongue Can Tell: Discover Your Sense of Taste.** Millbrook Press, 2000.

Hartley, Karen, Chris Macro, and Philip Taylor. **Tasting in Living Things.** Heinemann Library, 2000.

Molter, Carey. **Sense of Taste.** Abdo Publishing, 2001.

Nelson, Robin. **Tasting.** Lerner Publications Co., 2002.

Pringle, Laurence. **Explore Your Senses: Taste.** Marshall Cavendish, 2000.

Silverstein, Alvin, Virginia Silverstein, and Laura Silverstein Nunn. **Smelling and Tasting.** Twenty-First Century Books, 2002.

Viegas, Jennifer. **The Mouth and Nose: Learning How We Taste and Smell.** The Rosen Publishing Group, 2002.

Organizations and Online Sites

BodyQuest

http://library.thinkquest.org/ 10348/home.html

This site explores the human body's many different systems and parts.

How the Body Works

http://www.kidshealth.org

Learn all sorts of things about the health of your tongue, taste buds, and the rest of your body.

Human Anatomy Online

http://www.innerbody.com/ htm/body.html

Learn about the human body. See one hundred different images.

Neuroscience for Kids

http://faculty.washington. edu/chudler/chsense.html

Learn about all of five senses. Do fun things with your senses!

Important Words

digestive system the organs of the body that help digest or break down food so your body can use it

nasal cavity the space in your body where the organs of smell are located

nerve cell the smallest living thing that makes up the body's nerves and the nervous system

nerve fiber a thin fiber or tubelike material through which messages are sent between the brain and the spinal cord to let you see, hear, smell, taste, feel, and move

nerve impulse an electrical reaction sent along a nerve fiber to the brain

papillae bumps on the tongue that contain taste buds

saliva a liquid in your mouth that helps keep the mouth moist, helps make food soft, and starts the digestion process

Index

Meet the Author

Patricia J. Murphy writes children's storybooks, non-fiction books, early readers, and poetry. She also writes for magazines, corporations, educational publishing companies, and museums. She lives in Northbrook, IL. She especially likes the taste of warm, gooey chocolate chip cookies with milk!